Published

by

Great Yarmouth Local History and Archaeological Society

Third Reprint 2016

Printed
by
RPD Printers
Gorleston
Norfolk

HISTORIC
GREAT
YARMOUTH

by
Margaret Gooch

Great Yarmouth Local History and Archaeological Society

ISBN 978-0-9576092-1-1

The Great Yarmouth Local History and Archaeological Society

On 24th January 1888 a Great Yarmouth branch of the Norfolk and Norwich Archaeological Society was formed. On 27th February 1953, the Society became independent and its name was changed to the Great Yarmouth and District Archaeological Society. At the Annual General Meeting on 15th May 2009, it was decided to change the Society's name to the Great Yarmouth Local History and Archaeological Society in order to reflect members' changing interests.

The aims of the society are: to encourage the study of history and archaeology, especially in the Great Yarmouth District and to secure the preservation and conservation of historic buildings and monuments, within the Great Yarmouth District.

Its activities include lectures in the Northgate Room, Central Library, Tolhouse Street, Great Yarmouth at 7.30pm on the third Friday of each month, from January to May and from September to December. The lectures are on local, national, historical and archaeological topics.

At least two excursions are organised each summer, including a coach outing to a place of interest in East Anglia, and an evening visit to a village or a site.

The Society's journal is a compilation of articles, written mostly by local people, on local historical and archaeological topics, which is published each autumn.
The Society produces a quarterly newsletter, giving news of latest events, which is sent out to members, by email or by post.

The Society also erects blue plaques around the district to commemorate buildings, people and events of local interest.

Preface

This book is an updated version of "Historic Yarmouth", which was originally published in 1980 by the then Great Yarmouth and District Archaeological Society and was reprinted in 2001. The original book, as was stated in the introductory paragraphs, aimed to assist those who wished to explore Great Yarmouth, "behind the seafront". It listed the more outstanding features of the "old" town, i.e. Yarmouth within the town walls.

Since the first edition of the book, the Great Yarmouth Preservation Trust has come into being. It has saved a number of the historic buildings of the town, which have been restored and put to good use. Other regeneration projects have improved the historic environment of the town considerably. There has also been a growth in national interest in the Edwardian and Victorian buildings associated with English seaside, and several such buildings in Great Yarmouth have now been protected by listing.

This new edition is a guide to the historic buildings of Great Yarmouth and places them in the context of the history of the town. It continues to promote the aims of the original edition, but reflecting the advances in conservation, has included more historic buildings within the town walls, plus in a separate chapter, buildings beyond the wall which form part of Great Yarmouth's seaside and Naval heritage. The book has been structured in the form of two walks, with the features numbered and marked on the included map. The excellent drawings by Pat Page have been replaced by up -to-date photographs.

The Great Yarmouth Local History and Archaeological Society hopes that this book will provide a useful up-to-date guide for residents and visitors alike, and will generate interest in the heritage of this historic town.

Margaret Gooch.

Acknowledgements

The author wishes to thank those who have given considerable assistance in the writing and preparation of this book, particularly:

Dr. Paul Davies for editing and proof-reading.

Colin Tooke and Andrew Fakes for supplying information.

Derek Leak for taking the photographs.

CHAPTER ONE
THE OLD TOWN WITHIN THE WALLS

The walking tour of the old town of Great Yarmouth within the walls begins at the parish church of St. Nicholas.

The Great Yarmouth Minster Church of St. Nicholas (1) standing at the north end of the Market Place was founded in 1101 by Herbert de Losinga, Bishop of Norwich, as part of a penance. It was consecrated in 1119, the year of his death. As the prosperity and population of the port and town of Great Yarmouth rapidly increased, the church was enlarged three times. It was dedicated to St. Nicholas, the patron

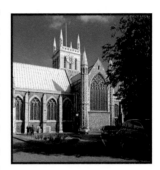

saint of sailors. St. Nicholas's is thought to be the largest parish church in England with a floor area of over 23,000 square feet, and possesses the widest aisles of any church in Europe. It retains its unique, long and narrow Norman ground plan within the later additions of the church. The only Norman work still to be seen is that on the lower stage of the tower, outside, just above the roofs. The upper part of the tower dates from 1200, whilst the parapet and pinnacles are Victorian. The church was gutted by fire-bombs in 1942 leaving only the walls and tower standing. The church was restored in 1957-60 to the designs of Stephen Dykes Bower.

Bartleman's Tombstone (2). In the south-west corner of the churchyard is the headstone, recently restored, which is inscribed, "He was the master of the brig Alexander and Margaret, who off the Norfolk coast with only three-pounders and ten men and boys, nobly defended himself against a cutter carrying 18 four-pounders and upwards of 100 men commanded by the notorious pirate Fall and fairly beat him off. Two hours later the enemy came down upon him again, when totally disabled, his mate Daniel McAuley expiring with loss of blood and himself dangerously wounded, was obliged to strike (the flag) and ransom. He brought his shattered vessel into Yarmouth with more than honours of a conqueror and died in consequence of his wounds on 14 February (1781)". The young Horatio Nelson was involved in patrols against Fall and other pirates and privateers.

The Old Vicarage (3) is the first building on the left when leaving the church gate. The oldest part of the house is a wing which dates from the 17th century. The southern part was built by the Corporation in 1718 and in 1781 it was extended into the churchyard. The windows are mostly 19th and 20th century. At one time, it was the home of Sir Astley Cooper, surgeon to Queen Victoria.

The Benedictine Priory (4) lies behind the Old Vicarage. Until its Dissolution in 1536, the Priory, a cell of the Benedictine Priory at Norwich Cathedral, served St. Nicholas's Church. It was rebuilt and enlarged in about 1260, at which time, the Great Hall (or Noble Hall) was added, which still

survives. The Hall is 60ft long and 30ft wide and retains many of its original features, including the site of the former screens passage with five archways on the west wall, leading to the former domestic offices It provided accommodation for some of the important visitors to Great Yarmouth, including royalty. After the

Dissolution, it fell into disuse, and later, for some time, was used as a stable. After the Suspension Bridge Disaster of 1845, when 79 people drowned, including many children from poor homes, funds were raised to improve the lot of the poor, and the Hall became a school. It is currently a community centre and café. (2013)

Sewell House (5) the birthplace of Anna Sewell, author of the book, "Black Beauty", is on the east side of the Market Place in Church Plain just to the south of the Old Vicarage. The house probably dates back to 1641, and though it appears to be timber-framed, the frontage was altered in 1932 when timbering, glass, brick and a mullioned window from an old building in one of Yarmouth's Rows were added. Originally it incorporated the neighbouring cottage on the south side, but it was divided into two separate dwellings in the 18th or 19th centuries

The Wrestlers' Inn (6) to the south, on Brewery Plain, was a 17th century inn famous for the many important people who stayed there. Part of it was destroyed by bombing in World War II and the remaining half of the building appears to have been partly rebuilt. When Nelson eventually returned to England on 6th November 1800, after the Battle of the Nile, he arrived at Great Yarmouth by packet boat. It was at the Wrestlers' Inn that he appeared at an upper window to greet the crowd, when he received the freedom of the town. When the Town Clerk asked him to place his right hand on the Bible to take the oath, he replied, "That, sir, is in Tenerife". It is now being used as an office building (2013).

The Market Place (7) covers 2¾ acres and is one of the largest open-air markets in England. As early as 1385 the area was paved and in that year the first Market Cross was erected. The third (and last) Market Cross was removed in 1836, when the

site was marked by a cruciform stone paving. Some of the buildings, particularly on the west side, are houses of 16th, 17th and 18th century origin, though this is disguised by their 20th century frontages. Being at the centre of the town, the market not only had a cross, but a cage, a pillory and stocks for punishing offending townsfolk, in particular, those vendors found guilty of giving short measure or selling bad produce. King Charles II granted a charter to the town in 1684 to hold two annual fairs, which were held in the Market Place; one in April and the other in August. By 1826, the August Fair had moved to Shrove Monday and Tuesday, and was known as the Cock Fair, as cock-fighting was one of its chief attractions. It ceased in 1891. The April Fair was at first held on Good Friday, but in 1715 it was moved to the Friday and Saturday following Easter. This fair continues to be held; a travelling fair still visits the town every year on the Friday and Saturday of Easter Week.

The Fishermen's Hospital (8) stands on the east side of the Market Place. It was founded by the Corporation in 1702 for old and "decayed" fishermen and their wives. It is a red brick building of one storey with dormers in the roof, built around an open courtyard paved with flint cobble stones. In the middle of the yard stands the statue of

Charity. The almshouses are approached by a gateway on the west side between two Dutch gables with large oval inscription boards surmounted by rich ornamental woodcarving with a motif of lions and roses. Opposite the gateway there is a semi-circular arched passage-way surmounted by a wooden cupola (with an ogee shaped roof) within which is a figure of St. Peter.

Miles Corbet's House (9). Further along, set back, is the house of Miles Corbet, who was the Recorder and Parliamentary Representative for the town, and Cromwell's personal friend and lawyer. He was the last of the 59 signatories on the death warrant of Charles I. After the Restoration of the Monarchy, Corbet was hung, drawn and quartered, and Pepys vividly described in the entry of his diary for 19th April 1662, that he saw Corbet and

others being taken to their execution and that they looked cheerful! The house is 17th century, brick, with an 18th century frontage, and has been a parish house and a tavern, and is currently (2013) a hairdresser's.

The Site of St Mary's Hospital (10). In the late 13th century the Hospital of St Mary was founded on the east side of the Market Place to care for the sick poor. After the Dissolution, the buildings were acquired by the Corporation, and in 1551 the Great Hall became the town's first Grammar School. In 1653, a charity school, educating 30 boys and 20 girls, and known as the Children's Hospital, was established in the old buildings. A new school, the Hospital School, was built on the site in 1843, and this was replaced in 1932 by the current building, which is now the St. Nicholas CE VC Priory Junior School.

Market Row (11) is on the west side of the Market Place; a narrow shopping Row with houses of 17th century origin. Some of the houses retain their original 17th century brick cellars. Number 8 was badly damaged by fire in 1995, but has been restored. Number 32 has an early 17th century window at the back. Numbers 31, 34 and 39 still have their warehouses at the rear.

Turn left into Howard Street to the **Friends' Meeting House, (12)** which was formerly an Austin Friary; a cell of the Austin Friary at Little Yarmouth, now part of Gorleston. The Quakers acquired the building in 1694, and although it has been altered, it still retains many original features, including a cellar (which may have been at street level originally), 17th century panelling, and part of a medieval doorway, which can be seen from the outside on the south wall. At the rear is a small garden, which is the Quaker burial ground.

Broad Row (13) to the west is a continuation of Market Row. Like Market Row, it is a narrow shopping Row, which again has a number of 17th century houses. Number 3 is a small 17th century house with a cellar and a brick fireplace. The first floor has panelling and the roof has four cruck trusses. Numbers 5, 11, 12 and 13 all have 17th century features.

Whitefriars (14). At the west end of Broad Row is the site of the Carmelite or Whitefriars Friary. In number 20 Broad Row, there is 15th century groin vaulted cellar, which is thought to have been part of the Friary. Whitefriars Court goes through to

Stonecutter's Way and from it can be seen a wall at the rear of number 26 Broad Row, with 16th century flint and brick. This is also thought to have belonged to the Friary or to have been constructed from material recovered from it.

Hall Quay (15) has a number of 16th, 17th and 18th century buildings, originally prestigious houses, generally with 19th and 20th century frontages, and later extensions to the rear.

The Duke's Head Hotel (16) is an early 17th century coaching inn, with knapped flint facing and Georgian windows. Inside, on the first floor, is a panelled room with a chimneypiece. In the rear coaching yard, a 14th century crown-post roof truss, which is from a medieval Guildhall that was on or near the site, is fixed to the wall.

The Star Hotel (17) is the former Cromwell (Temperance) Hotel. The original Star Hotel, next door to the south, was demolished to make way for the former post office in 1930, and its 16th century panelling was sold and is currently in the Metropolitan Museum in New York. The current Star Hotel was a single-storey 17th century building. In the 1890's, when it

was being converted into the Cromwell Hotel, the timbered upper floors and the enclosed balcony were added. There is 18th century panelling in the front lounge, which possibly comes from the demolished hotel next door. There is a modern extension at the rear.

The Haven Bridge (18) over the River Yare, was opened in 1930 by the Prince of Wales, later Edward VIII and the Duke of Windsor. It replaced a series of six previous bridges, the first of which was constructed in 1417, and had replaced a ferry.

The Ice House (19), on the south west side of the bridge, is thatched and constructed of gault brick, was one of two built in 1859-62, (the other was demolished). They stored ice taken from the Broads and imported from Scandinavia, for use in the fishing industry.

The Town Hall (20) was constructed in 1882, replacing the Georgian Town Hall, which had faced the river. In red brick, with terracotta detail and a red sandstone basement storey, the hall has a clock tower some 110 feet tall. The handsome Assembly Hall occupies most of the first floor. In 1886, the building began to subside towards the west, and the clock tower began to lean, so the west side of the building was underpinned with steel girders and concrete.

The South Quay (21). Proceed along this once-elegant tree-lined quayside, with fine houses, a few of which remain. Daniel Defoe described it as "the finest quay in Europe, and not inferior to Marseilles"!

The Elizabethan House, Number 4 South Quay (22). The house was built in 1596 for Benjamin Cooper, a wealthy merchant,

and the town's Member of Parliament and a Bailiff. John Carter, a Parliamentarian, purchased the house in 1635, where he was visited by Oliver Cromwell, General Ireton and Miles Corbet, and it is said, that the decision to execute Charles I was taken here. C. J. Palmer, the local antiquarian, lived in the house in the early 19th century. The house was originally one room deep, but between 1603 and 1610, it was extended to the rear. In 1610, Cooper was licensed to build over Row 83. On the ground floor there are examples of 16th and 18th century panelling, and in the dining room, there is an arcaded fireplace with Benjamin Cooper's initials and the date 1596. The central first-floor room has a 16th century plaster ceiling, and a further room has another arcaded fireplace with Cooper's initials, and 17th century panels. The six-bay Georgian façade of gault brick dates from Palmer's occupancy. The house is owned by the National Trust and is managed by Norfolk Museums Service. It is currently open to the public (2013).

Numbers 5 and 6 South Quay (23) date from the mid-18th century and have stick baluster staircases. **Numbers 7 and 8 (24)** are early 19th century, and **Number 11 (25)** was originally built in 1660 and reconstructed also in the early 19th century.

Greyfriars (26). From Row 92, the ruins of the Franciscan Friary can be viewed. It was founded here most likely before 1270, and the precinct stretched from the river to Middlegate Street and from Row 83 to Row 96. The Friary was suppressed in 1538, by Richard Ingworth, and acquired by John Woodroffe in 1657, who drove a road, now Queen Street, through the precinct on the site of the nave of the former Friary church. In the 16th century, some of the Friary buildings were converted into houses, and later uses for parts of the site included an orchard, a militia training yard and a school. The bombing of this area in 1941-2, exposed the ruins of the Friary, which we can see today. Four bays of the cloister survive and it has the distinction of being the only surviving vaulted Franciscan cloister in the United Kingdom. Tudor fireplaces and wooden mullioned window frames can still be seen in the ruins, and tomb recesses with limestone canopies survive at the back of a fireplace, together with medieval tomb slabs. There are the remains of a high-quality wall-painting dated at about 1310 on the back of the west tomb recess. The ruins are in the care of English Heritage, and are occasionally open to the public (2013).

Number 13 South Quay (27) is an 18th century brick house.

Numbers 16 and 17 (28) date from about 1825.

The Old Custom House, No 20 South Quay (29) is a very fine house which was built c. 1720 for John Andrews, once described as "the greatest herring merchant in Europe". The house was acquired by the Crown in 1802 for use as the Custom House, and in 1985, became the headquarters of the Great Yarmouth Port Authority. It is of red brick with stone trim, with a porch with Greek Doric columns added in c. 1802. It has large-framed panelling on the ground floor, a staircase with barley sugar and iron-twist balusters, and the boardroom on the first floor, has a ribbed plaster ceiling and small-framed panelling.

The Dutch Chapel, site of (30). Turn left towards the library. A plaque on the wall to the left commemorates the Dutch Chapel, a 16th century building, which had been used as a prayer room by Dutch refugees, and later as a warehouse. It was destroyed by enemy bombing in 1942. The site is now the car park and access road to the library, which was built in 1961.

The Tolhouse (31). Attached to the library is the Tolhouse, built in flint, originally as a private house, and is the oldest secular building in the town. It was in public use by the 13th century, and has been owned by the Borough since 1552. There are the remains of a Norman arch at the ground floor beneath the Great Hall, which indicates a 12th century origin. The Great Hall on the first floor is approached by an external stairway from the street. The main entrance door is Early English with dog-tooth decoration and moulded capitals. The building has been used a court, a warehouse, municipal offices, a gaol, a police station and a library. In the basement there are four 18th century prison cells, which were in use until the late 19th century. The building was severely damaged in World War II, and was restored in 1960. It is currently (2013) a museum. Now return to the Quay and head south.

Row 111 House and the Old Merchant's House (Row 117) (32). Both are early 17th century houses, which were bombed in 1942 and subsequently re-built. An architectural team investigated the ruined houses in this heavily bombed area of old Great Yarmouth, and found the remains of many 17th century houses, most of which were beyond restoration. The investigators

removed doors, fireplaces, panelling and anything else of interest, including Delft tiles and wall anchors from ruined buildings for use in restoring the Row 111 House and the Old Merchant's House. Both houses are built of brick and flint with mullioned windows. Row 111 House had been divided in the 19th century into three dwellings, which was typical of how fine row houses declined into slums. The house has 18th century panelling and a shell-cupboard. The Old Merchant's House has impressive 17th century plaster ceilings, which survived the bombing, including an early royal coat of arms of James 1. Articles removed from bombed houses are on display in both houses, which are museums (2013) in the care of English Heritage.

26 South Quay, currently (2013) The Nelson Museum (33) was formerly the home of Sir George England, Mayor and Member of Parliament, and a supporter of the Parliamentarian cause in the Civil War. It is 17th century, with an early 19th century Georgian façade.

Turn left into Nottingham Way and on the corner with King Street, stands an early 17th century building, the former **White Lion Inn (34)**. It is constructed in flint and brick, and inside there is a 17th century staircase and rooms with small-framed panelling. It is currently (2013) being converted into housing.

Turn right into King Street. Many houses along this street are of 17th century origin with later facades. **St. Spiridon's Church (35)** (Greek Orthodox) is the former St. Peter's Church, which was built in 1831. When St. Nicholas's Church was bombed in World War II, it became the

Parish Church until St. Nicholas's was restored in 1957-60. Continue south along King Street to Friars Lane, where part of the town's medieval walls can be seen.

The Town Wall (36). Henry III gave permission in 1261 for a wall and ditch to be constructed. The wall was begun in 1285 and completed by 1396. The medieval town was confined within these

walls. They were constructed on three sides, with the long north-south wall facing the sea, and many of the buildings between the walls and the sea date from the 18th and 19th C. There was no wall facing the riverside, and at that time there were no bridges into the town across the rivers Yare and Bure until 1417; the only crossings were ferries. There was therefore, no direct river crossing into the town; a defensive boom was stretched across the river to protect it from attack by that route. The walls are recorded as being 23 feet high with 18 towers and ten gates (the main gates were at the north and south). The inner wall has brick arcading supporting a wall-walk. The towers were either D-shaped or circular, except one. The walls are remarkably complete; eleven towers remain, but the gates were demolished in the 18th and early 19th centuries, to make room for wider waggons.

Blackfriars Priory, site of (37). The Dominican Priory or Blackfriars was founded here in 1271. The site stretched the length of Friars Lane and was bounded on the south and east sides by the town wall. The Priory was burned down in 1525; and nothing remains on the site.

Blackfriars Tower (38). Proceed into Trinity Place, walk beside the wall and pass through Blackfriars Tower. The passage way through the tower was made in 1807.

Turn right into Mariners Road along the wall to **Palmer's Tower (39)** and continue to the main road. The wall continues towards the river, behind some buildings, and originally extended to the river's edge, where the South Mount was built (now completely destroyed).

If you turn right on to Southgates Road, you will see a green plaque marking where the **South Gate or Great Gate (40)** (demolished in 1812) straddled South Quay. The defensive boom

21

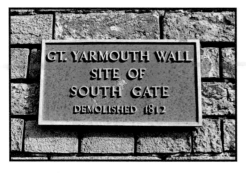

was stretched across the river near here.

Return to Blackfriars Tower and turn left into Blackfriars Road and continue to the **South-East Tower (41)**. It is

D-shaped with brick and flint chequer work, a 19th century structure on the roof and a 14th century lower stage. Against the tower and built into the wall, is an early 19th century fish curing works, which is now (2013) a pottery. With the wall on the left, pass the Old Jewish Cemetery and the site of the **Garden Gate (42)**, which was demolished in 1808.

The Time and Tide Museum (43) is on the right, and is the

former Tower Fish Curing Works. Great Yarmouth's origins and prosperity depended on herring fishing from the tenth century until the collapse of the industry in the mid-twentieth century, owing to over-fishing and a decline in the markets. In the 19th century, herring were smoked, cured or pickled for export, and the numbers of curing works expanded greatly. At the curing works, fish were washed, dry-salted and placed in steeps of brine pickle. The fish were then "rived", or threaded, on sticks known as "speets", which were placed on racks or "loves" in the smokehouse. The Tower Curing Works was built in 1880, at the peak of the town's herring fishing trade and closed in 1987 after the decline and collapse of herring fishing. The works were acquired by Great Yarmouth Preservation Trust in 1988. A £5 million project restored the buildings and refurbished them as the Time and Tide Museum, a major cultural, educational and tourism resource for the town. The buildings are in red brick; the north front has groups of shuttered vents under the eaves and on the inside, the "loves" have remained in place. The red brick manager's house also survives near the entrance.

Continuing along Blackfriars Road, walk behind the church, cross St. Peter's Road, the site of the **Ropemakers' Gate (44)**, demolished in 1785, and proceed along an unnamed passage running between Deneside and St. Peter's Plain. This gives the best view of the wall to the left with houses on King Street built into it, including **Harris's Tower (45),** which has part of a house

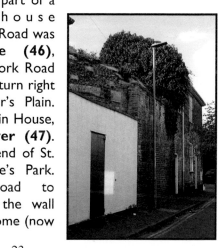

built on to its base. At York Road was the **Little Mount Gate (46)**, demolished in 1804. Cross York Road and continue along a passage, turn right and then left into St. Peter's Plain. Look at the wall behind Ravelin House, the site of the **Ravelin Tower (47)**. Return and proceed to the end of St. Peter's Plain, to St. George's Park. Turn left, and cross the road to Alexandra Road, and note the wall behind the former Nurses' Home (now

23

flats), and the remains of the **Shave Tower (48),** and here is the site of the **New Gate or Chapel Gate (49),** demolished in 1789.

To the left is **St George's Church (50)**. It was erected in 1714 by the Corporation as a chapel-of-ease for St. Nicholas's Church. The construction was paid for by a local coal tax. It was made redundant

in the 1950's and was found to be structurally unsound in 2006. A Georgian gem, Grade I listed, the church has been restored for use as a theatre and arts centre. During restoration works, paint finishes of national historic importance on the internal pillars were discovered.

Proceed along Alexandra Road; the wall can be seen in places to the rear of the houses on the left,

including the **Pinnacle Tower (51)**. Proceed to the end of Alexandra Road and turn left. The wall runs between shops, and above, there are a few decorative flints marking the position of the wall. A green plaque commemorates the **Oxney Gate (52)**, also known as the Theatre Gate, which was demolished in 1778. Cross to the Market Gates Shopping Centre.

A passage runs north between shops. Proceed along it, and from the elevated walkway, there is an interesting view of the rampart walk and the **Guard Tower (53)**. At the end of the passage turn immediately right and walk back behind the wall to view the other side of the elevated wall walk (very good flint facing) and the

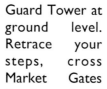

Guard Tower at ground level. Retrace your steps, cross Market Gates Road, passing the site of the **Market Gate (54)**, demolished in 1830, to the second-hand furniture shop (2013). You can see the wall and the **Hospital Tower (55)** behind the shop, but a better view

and access to the Tower can be had by following the shop round to the main road, and turning into Fisher's Court to see the wall at the back, and the Tower.

Return to the main road; there is more wall at the back of the car park. Cross the road to

Sainsbury's and walk alongside the wall at the back of Sainsbury's car park. Cross the churchyard by taking the path to the east of the main porch of Great Yarmouth Minster, to **King Henry's Tower (56)**, thought to have been the first tower to be built, probably soon after 1285. It is octagonal (the only tower which is this shape) in flint with limestone corner stones. The wall turns left to form part of the boundary of the churchyard. Exit the churchyard through the gate to the right of King Henry's Tower and turn left into Ferrier Road and pass the North East Tower. Proceed along Town Wall Road, passing the site of the **North Gate (57)**, cross Northgate Street and into

Rampart Road. The wall continued along the middle of Rampart Road, and a bump along the middle of the road can still be seen, and presumably there are some foundations still there. **The North-West Tower (58)** (and the end of the wall) is across the road on North Quay beside the river Bure.

CHAPTER TWO
GREAT YARMOUTH OUTSIDE THE WALLS

Start on the seafront at the end of Regent Road on the Marine Parade, facing the sea.

The Marine Parade (59). Along the seashore at Great Yarmouth there was originally a fishing community and there were very few buildings east of the Town Wall until the early 19th century. Building on this land, called the Denes, was severely restricted until 1810. Restrictions were relaxed in 1835, as visiting the seaside increased in popularity, at first among the better-off, who came for taking the waters, bathing in salt water and breathing the ozone. The seafront began to be developed and the Marine Parade was first

constructed in 1857. With the coming of the railways and the passing of the 1871 Bank Holiday Act, trips to the seaside ceased to be the preserve of the gentry and middle classes and thousands of working people began to enjoy seaside visits. Building along the seafront and in the network of new roads to the west of it, grew apace. In 1877, the Marine Parade was widened by 60 feet. At the junction of Regent Road and the Marine Parade, the **New Beach Hotel (60)**, (formerly the Queen's Hotel), was built in 1880.

The Hollywood Cinema (61). At the north end of the Marine Parade stands the Hollywood Cinema, which occupies the former Aquarium building. The original Aquarium was built on the site of one of the town's gun batteries and was opened in 1876. It boasted 18 large tanks plus ponds, which housed a variety of fish, alligators and seals. There was a reading room, a roller skating rink on the roof and an open-air theatre. The Prince of Wales (later Edward VII) visited and, in 1881, attended a concert here, but the complex went bankrupt later that year. In 1883, the new Royal Aquarium, (acquiring the prefix "Royal", reflecting the Prince's interest) was built. It was constructed in gault brick with a terracotta façade, and opened as a theatre, with some aquaria retained. There was a Grand Hall, where touring variety shows were staged, a restaurant and a Minor Hall for smaller performances. From 1954, resident summer shows were held in the main hall and the smaller hall became the Little Theatre, where in the late 20th century, repertory companies performed plays. In 1970, it became a cinema, the Royalty, and is now, in 2013, the Hollywood Cinema.

The Britannia Pier (62). The first purpose-built pier to be constructed in Great Yarmouth, was the Wellington Pier in 1853. This proved to be a popular success, and in 1858, another, the Britannia Pier,

aligned with Regent Road, was opened. The only buildings allowed on it were bathing, reading and refreshment rooms, (no shops) plus a tollhouse and a lighthouse. It was constructed in timber, but in 1867 the pier was cut in two during a gale by a schooner, and after repair, another schooner sliced through it in 1878. It was demolished in 1900 and the new Britannia Pier, constructed in timber and steel, was opened in 1902. It was 810 feet long, with a grand pavilion seating 1,200 people at the eastern end. Shops were now allowed. In 1909, fire destroyed the pavilion, followed by another in 1914, probably started by the Suffragettes, and further fires in 1932 and 1954 destroyed not only the pavilion again, but the ballroom as well. The current pavilion was built in 1958. Big name shows have performed on the pier since 1950.

The Empire, the site of Ansell's buildings (63). The Empire Picture Playhouse opened in 1911 and remained a cinema until 1991. It became a bingo hall and then a theme bar. It was built on the site of Ansell's Buildings; the first to be used as a seaside lodging house in the town in the early 19th century. Lodging houses then began to appear along the seafront. The Empire is currently unoccupied (2013).

The Sailors' Home now the Tourist Information Centre (64). In the days of sail, the coast off Great Yarmouth was extremely dangerous. Shipwrecks were common and in 1858, a meeting was held with a view to building a Sailors' Home to provide accommodation, rest and care for shipwrecked sailors of all nations, who were brought ashore, and for those paid-off or waiting to join a ship. In 1859, the Home was opened in temporary buildings behind the Bath Hotel and, in 1861, after extensive fund-raising, the new building was opened on Marine Parade. In addition to board and lodging, the Home proved a library, museum, charts and training for apprentices. It finally closed in 1965, and has since been a Maritime Museum and is now (2013) the Tourist Information Centre.

St. John's Church (65). (Along York Road). The church, which was opened in 1858, was built for the Beach and Harbour Mission, which served the needs of the beachmen and their families. The pews were reserved for the fishing families. St. John's was built of flint, stone and brick, in the Early English style. There are six nave arcades with low round

columns. The capitals are decorated with stiff leaf, seaweed and shell designs. The church has been enlarged and altered at various times, and is at present (2013) closed and awaiting restoration.

The Flamingo Amusement Arcade, the site of the Old Bath House and the Bath Hotel (66). The supposed medicinal

benefits of sea water were proclaimed in the 18th century and "Taking the Waters" became fashionable among the upper and middle classes. In Great Yarmouth a new Bath House was constructed in 1759-60 on the site of what is now the Flamingo Amusement Arcade. It consisted of two large sea-water plunge baths; one for ladies and one for gentlemen, with dressing rooms. It became popular and a large assembly room was added to the premises, where the discerning visitors enjoyed concerts, balls, tea parties, breakfasts and playing billiards. In 1835, the Bath House was rebuilt and enlarged. The old baths were removed, and new, smaller baths were installed, giving the choice of hot or cold sea water. Lodgings were provided and it became known as the Bath Hotel.

The Hippodrome Circus (67).
Set slightly back from Marine Parade is George Gilbert's Hippodrome Circus, which was opened in 1903. George Gilbert, and his wife, Jennie O'Brien, performed a bare-back equestrian circus act all over the world. When they came to Great

Yarmouth in 1898, a small wooden circus building was constructed for the show. George Gilbert replaced this building with the present one, which is constructed of concrete, with a terracotta façade by R. S. Cockrill, and Art Nouveau features. The stables of the old Bath Hotel were demolished to improve the view of the new building from the promenade. The building incorporates a sinking circus ring, one of only three remaining in the world, which fills with 60,000 gallons of water to provide a spectacular aquatic show as part of the circus performance. Much of the original equipment is still in use today, with circus shows including water spectaculars performed for the summer and Christmas seasons.

The Jetty, site of (69). The Jetty was originally constructed in 1560 for landing fish and for loading and unloading cargo. The river outlet to the sea continually silted up and the Jetty, which had a crane at the east end, provided a reliable means of loading and unloading boats. It was rebuilt in 1701 and was damaged in 1767 and in 1791. During the Napoleonic Wars, the Royal Naval Fleet frequently assembled in Yarmouth Roads, because ships would be too vulnerable to siege or attack in the harbour. Officers, men and stores were loaded from the Jetty as ships were replenished before sailing. In 1801, Nelson sailed from the Jetty with the Fleet to the Battle of Copenhagen. After the Battle, prisoners and the wounded were landed at the Jetty. Nelson then landed there to visit the wounded at the Hospital for the Sick and Wounded of the Army and Navy, which was then roughly where Sainsbury's is today (2013). The Jetty was rebuilt in 1809 at the cost of £5,000, a considerable sum in those days, emphasising its importance to the town. (The town tried to recover the sum from the Royal Navy, citing damage during the wars). In the late 19th and early 20th centuries, when Great Yarmouth became a seaside destination, the Jetty became popular for promenading; trippers boarded steamers from it, and fishermen continued to land their catches there. During the Second World War, there was a gun emplacement at the east end and part of the Jetty was demolished for fear of invasion. In 1961, the timber structure was reinforced with metal, and gradually the Jetty fell into disrepair. The Council was not prepared to fund the repair of this important example of the town's heritage at a cost of £350,000 and spent some £90,000 on demolishing it in 2011. A plaque marks the site.

The Windmill Theatre (68) with its twin towers, terracotta façade, and windmill sails, was formerly the Gem Cinema, the first purpose-built cinema in the town, which opened in 1908. It remained a cinema until it closed in 1939. It was re-opened in 1946 as the Windmill Theatre, presenting big-name summer shows. These ended in the 1980's and since then it has been used respectively as a children's fun house, Ripley's Believe It or Not, a waxworks and as an indoor golf course.

The First Hotels and Elegant Terraces (70). The first hotel to be built along the seafront was the Royal Hotel in 1840, where Charles Dickens wrote parts of David Copperfield. In 1841, the

Victoria Building Company began an ambitious development plan to build terraces of elegant houses to encourage the middle classes to live in the town. The Victoria Hotel, now the Carlton Hotel, was built in 1842, and later spread to take

in some of Kimberley Terrace, which had been constructed in 1849. Leading off the Marine Parade to the west, Camperdown, a terrace of smaller elegant houses, which have recently been restored, was built soon after, together with Brandon Terrace and Albert Square. The development scheme did not proceed and there was no further construction from the plans. The Wellington Arches, which were supposed to be the gateway to the scheme, remain behind the terraces. Many of these terraced large private houses along the Marine Parade became boarding houses.

The Winter Gardens (71) was originally constructed in Torquay in 1878-81. It was purchased by Great Yarmouth Corporation for a bargain price of £1,300 and re-erected on its current site in 1903. It is a glass structure, iron-framed with timber window surrounds and traditional lattice girders. It was long-used as a roller skating rink. In 1966, it became the Biergarten, and then a night club. It is currently closed (2013) and awaiting restoration.

The Wellington Pier (72); the first purpose-built pier, was constructed in 1853. The Duke of Wellington had died in 1852 and it was decided to build the pier in his memory. Seaside piers

were at first landing stages for steamers and boat trips, but soon became popular for promenading and entertainment. The pier was 700 feet long and had a small building at the east end. Military bands and concert parties provided entertainment. It was considerably altered in 1900, when the Great Yarmouth Corporation bought it, and in 1903, the pavilion by J. W. Cockrill, was added. Variety shows were staged there throughout the 20th century and, in the 1960's and 70's, top-name stars performed there in the summer season.

The Assembly Rooms, now the Masonic Lodge (73) was built in 1863 and provided both assembly rooms and a reading room. It was used as the Officers' Mess for the Prince of Wales Own Norfolk Artillery. The Prince of Wales (later Edward

VII) was their Colonel and often visited the officers there.

The Shadingfield Lodge now the Grosvenor Casino (74) was built as a seaside lodge for the Cuddon family of Suffolk. The Cuddon's were friends of the Prince of Wales, who stayed there eight times.

The Pleasure Beach with the Scenic Railway (75). In 1889, a Sinuous Railway and Toboggan Slide were built to the south of the Pleasure Beach, nearly opposite the Royal Naval Hospital. In 1909, Great

Yarmouth Amusements Ltd. acquired the lease of a site on the beach for a Scenic Railway and two sideshows. The Railway opened in July that year, together with the Katzenjammer Castle and the Merry Widow Waltzer. In May 1910, the

River Caves were constructed under the Scenic Railway. In 1912, the framework of the Scenic Railway was encased in quick-drying plaster to give a mountain effect, complete with snow-capped peaks, after which it was known as the Royal Mountain Scenic Railway. It was destroyed by fire in 1919, but was quickly rebuilt. More rides were added and, by 1929, the site was known as the Pleasure Beach. A new, large rollercoaster, built and designed by Eric Heidrich for the Colonial Exhibition, was purchased in 1932 and brought to the Pleasure Beach in that year to replace the existing one. The Scenic Railway is the only remaining wooden one of its kind in the United Kingdom, and one of only eight in the world. The Pleasure Beach continued to grow post-war and the site now covers nine acres and has 70 rides and attractions.

The Royal Naval Hospital (76) was built in 1809-11 for casualties of the Napoleonic Wars. It replaced the earlier hospital, which was situated roughly where Sainsbury's is today

(2013). It was constructed of the finest materials by Miles and Peto, at a cost of £120,000 (a considerable sum then). The design is quadrangular and has four ranges constructed in yellow stock brick, which were large ward blocks. The gatehouse is formed as a triumphal arch with Tuscan pilasters. The Hospital became a barracks, but reverted to being a hospital when the Royal Naval Arsenal was built in Southtown. It has been an army hospital, a naval asylum, a World War II naval base headquarters and an N.H.S. psychiatric hospital. It has now been sympathetically converted into apartments.

The Norfolk Pillar, Nelson's Monument, 1817-19 (77). After Nelson's death, the town went into mourning. An appeal was launched throughout Norfolk so that a monument could be erected in his memory. The foundation stone was laid on 15th August 1815. The monument is 144 feet high, (a little shorter than the one in Trafalgar Square, but was built some 30 years earlier). The column is in the style of the Greek Doric order with caryatides and Britannia holding a trident and a laurel wreath. The figures were originally in Coade stone, but were replaced, first by concrete replicas and then by glass fibre. The monument was restored in 1984.

Bibliography

Davies, Paul P., *The Beach and Harbour Mission, the Beachmen's Church, St. John's Church, Great Yarmouth,* Paul Davies, (2011).

Davies, Paul, (ed.) *Excerpt from Great Yarmouth Sailors' Home Log Book,* GYLHAS, (2011).

Davies, Paul P., *The Parish Church of St. Nicholas,* Paul Davies, (2007).

Defoe, Daniel, *Tour Through the Eastern Counties,* (1724).

Hedges, A.A.C., *Yarmouth is an Antient Town,* Great Yarmouth Corporation, (1959).

Hunt, Alan, (comp.), *Plaques in and Around Great Yarmouth and Gorleston,* edited by Gooch, Margaret and Davies, Paul, GYLHAS, (2013).

Palmer, C. J., *The Perlustration of Great Yarmouth,* 3 vols, (1875). Pepys, Samuel, *The Shorter Pepys,* edited by Latham, Robert, Penguin, (1987).

Pevsner, Nikolaus, and Wilson, Bill, *The Buildings of England: Norfolk 1: Norwich and the North-East,* Penguin Books, (1997).

Riley, Bronwen, *Great Yarmouth Row Houses and Greyfriars' Cloister,* English Heritage, (2011).

Tooke, Colin, *The Broad Row: Great Yarmouth,* Colin Tooke, (2012).

Tooke, Colin, *Great Yarmouth and the Nelson Connection,* Colin Tooke, (2005).

Tooke, Colin, *Great Yarmouth and Gorleston: Beside the Sea,* Tookes Books, (2001).

Tooke, Colin, *Great Yarmouth: The Rows and the Old Town,* Tookes Books, (2000).

Tooke, Colin, *Shops and Shopping,* Colin Tooke, (2010).